D1241402

Everything
HORSE

What Kids Really Want to Know About Horses

by
Marty Crisp

NorthWord
Minnetonka, Minnesota

Edited by Ruth Strother
Designed by Lois A. Rainwater
Design concept by Michele Lanci-Altomare

Text © 2005 by Marty Crisp

NorthWord

Books for Young Readers
11571 K-Tel Drive
Minnetonka, MN 55343
www.tnkidsbooks.com

The horses in this book are referred to as *he* unless gender is known.

Photographs © 2005 provided by:
Alamy/John Foxx: pp. 1, 25, 57; Alamy/Ingram Publishing: p. 8;
Alamy/Apis Abramis: pp. 22, 26-27;
Alamy/Juniors Bildarchiv: pp. 36-37, 47; Alamy/Dominis John: p. 54;
Comstock.com: pp. 11, 42; Fotosearch.com/Corel: cover (all except top left),
back cover, pp. 3, 5, 13, 15-21, 24, 28-29, 32, 33, 34 (far left and far right), 35
(far left and middle), 44-45, 50, 51, 58-59, 60 (upper left); Getty Images/Digital Vision: pp. 6 (upper right), 7, 34 (middle), 38-39, 40,
53, 56, 60 (upper right and bottom); Getty Images/Photodisc: cover (top
left), pp. 4, 31, 35 (far right), 55, 61, 62; Getty Images/Brand X: p. 41 (pony);
Punchstock/Corbis: p. 6 (upper left); Punchstock/Brand X: p. 6 (bottom);
Punchstock/Photodisc: pp. 14, 41 (mule), 49 (woman);
Punchstock/Thinkstock: pp. 48-49 (horseshoes).

Illustration © 2005 by Michael Langham Rowe: p. 8 (hoof)

Library of Congress Cataloging-in-Publication Data

Crisp, Marty.
Everything horse : what kids really want to know about horses / by Marty
Crisp.
p. cm. — (Kids' faqs)
ISBN 1-55971-920-6 (hardcover) — ISBN 1-55971-921-4 (softcover)
1. Horses--Miscellanea—Juvenile literature. I. Title. II. Series.

SF302.C75 2005
636.1--dc22   2004024134

Printed in Singapore
10 9 8 7 6 5 4 3 2

Acknowledgments

I COULDN'T HAVE WRITTEN THIS BOOK WITHOUT THE help of Stephanie Shertzer Lawson, editor/publisher of *Pennsylvania Equestrian* and a passionate advocate for horses. Special thanks also to Jeffrey M. Edelson, VMD, PC, of Edelson Equine Associates with its state-of-the-art equine hospital in Manheim, PA. His patient answers and expert read-through were invaluable. And for many of the great questions, thanks to the first through eighth grade students and their teacher, Annie Stauffer, at West Terre Hill School, an Old Order Mennonite one-room schoolhouse in Lancaster County, PA.

Dedication

With love to the fine fillies my sons recently married:
Heidi Bordner Crisp, Lorilee Darrow Crisp, and Katie
Linsky Crisp. You're all blue ribbon champions,
and we're proud to have you in our corral.

—M. C.

contents

Horses have been friends and helpers
to people for centuries.

introduction

LONG AGO, PRIMITIVE MEN HUNTED HORSES for food. Then a caveman with some imagination figured out that horses could be put to better use. At first, horses carried heavy packs and loads of wood. As time went by, horses were harnessed to pull carts, wagons, carriages, plows, barges, and even firefighting equipment. They turned wheels to grind grain, rounded up cattle, and delivered the mail.

At the same time, the horse proved itself to be one of earth's most courageous animals. A New York City policeman and his horse forgot their own safety and rescued 20 frightened circus horses from a flaming tent. And a New Zealand horse named Moifaa survived a shipwreck and swam 20 miles (32 km) to land. Then just weeks after being rescued, Moifaa won the world's most demanding cross-country race.

An estimated 60 million domestic horses exist today. Horse racing has its own TV channel, and horse shows and expos draw many thousands of fans annually. A Canadian radio broadcaster once said of the champion racer Northern Dancer, "he runs a hole in the wind." That is, indeed, what horses do.

Parts of a horse

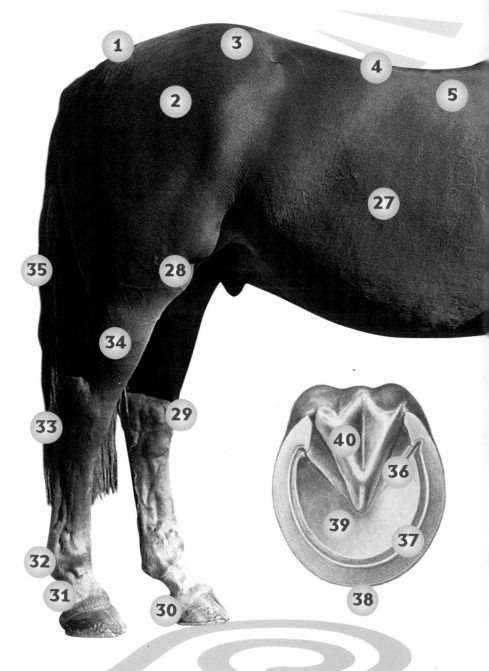

1. Dock
2. Hindquarter
3. Croup
4. Loins
5. Back
6. Withers
7. Neck
8. Crest
9. Mane
10. Poll
11. Ear
12. Forehead
13. Eye
14. Nostril
15. Muzzle
16. Lower jaw
17. Cheek
18. Chest
19. Elbow
20. Right foreleg

21. Knee
22. Cannon bone
23. Fetlock
24. Coronet
25. Hoof
26. Chestnut
27. Flank
28. Stifle
29. Hock
30. Heel
31. Pastern
32. Ergot
33. Point of hock
34. Gaskin
35. Tail
36. Bar
37. White line
38. Hoof wall
39. Sole
40. Frog

Did horses come from dinosaurs?

Like most mammals, horses came after the dinosaurs. The earliest horse fossils date back about 50 million years and were found in North America. This seems odd, since history books tell us Europeans brought the first horses to the Americas. But 50 million years ago, planet Earth was one large land mass, which later separated into continents divided by oceans.

You wouldn't have recognized the very first horse, *Hyracotherium*. It was about the size of a lamb, and it had four toes on each of its front feet and three on its back feet. As the earth's climate changed and steamy swamps gave way to grassy plains, the horse changed, too. Its legs became longer for running and the toes on each foot grew together and became one hoof. The horse kept growing larger, and its legs and face got longer. About 15 million years ago, the hoofed animal we know today as *Equus* looked much as it does now. The word *equine* comes form the horse's scientific name *Equus,* and means relating to horses.

Starting around 3000 B.C., people from roaming tribes of central Asia were the first to domesticate the horse and use it as a pulling animal. Wherever people went, those with horses brought them along. In the sixteenth century, the Spanish conquistadors landed on the shores of Central America and reintroduced the horse to the very place it had come from so long ago. When the Aztecs first saw the Spaniards on horseback, they fell back in awe, sure that man and horse were one magical creature.

Horses are herd animals and enjoy being in the company of other horses.

Why were horses used in warfare?

Men needed them. In Roman times, warriors rode in horse-drawn chariots. Then warriors learned to ride bareback and the Persian Empire developed the first horse cavalry. This gave the Persians a huge advantage, since a single horse is much easier to turn and move around than a chariot.

Horses became so important in battle that they wore their own armor. By the end of the 1700s, though, bullets and cannonballs were used in war and armor became useless. Yet horses continued to charge into battle in cavalry units until automatic weapons and shrapnel were invented in the late 1800s.

By the end of World War I (1914–1918), mechanical transport like jeeps, trucks, and tanks finally took the horse's place, and horses stopped dying in battle. They still serve in many countries' armed services, but today they're used mainly for ceremonial purposes.

The Royal Canadian Mounted Police ride their horses in a parade.

Riding is a popular sport and requires lots of equipment, unless you're riding bareback.

Why are horses mounted from the left?

A lot of what's done in the horse world is based on tradition. Mounting from the left falls under that category and dates back to the days of knights in shining armor. Most knights, like most people today, were right-handed. They wore their sword on their left side so they could easily reach across with their right hand and pull the sword smoothly out of the scabbard (sword holster). The last thing a knight wanted to do when trying to mount a horse was to swat him accidentally on the side with the scabbard. Modern riders don't wear armor, but the tradition of mounting horses from the left lives on.

Skirt, fender, cantle, and stirrups are all parts of a typical saddle.

What was the Pony Express?

On April 3, 1860, in Saint Joseph, Missouri, a crowd gathered to watch a history-making event: the start of the Pony Express. The telegraph had been invented, but there was no cross-country line yet. Since there was also no cross-country railroad or stagecoach line, mail was slowly delivered from coast to coast by pioneers in wagons or by steamships. It took four months in 1841 for Californians

to get the news that President William Henry Harrison had died in Washington, D.C.

So a group of freight company owners decided to offer 10-day mail delivery using a horse-and-rider relay. They rounded up a herd of 400 small mustangs to be ridden by jockey-sized mail carriers as young as 15. Each rider traveled 75–100 miles (121–161 km), changing horses about every 15 miles (24 km). The Express route ran from Missouri to California, passing through Kansas, Nebraska, Colorado, Wyoming, Utah, and Nevada.

Pony Express couriers carried no more than 20 pounds (9 kg) of mail. They could gallop a distance of more than 2,000 miles (3,218 km) in 11 days. The Pony Express boys rode across deserts and through dust storms, downpours, blizzards, and snowy mountain passes.

Are horses the most important animal in history?

No animal in human history has done more physical work for people than the horse. Native Americans recognized the value of a horse as soon as they saw one. When Europeans brought the first horses to America, natives were willing to trade land, handiwork, and even women for these magnificent beasts. Native Americans are still known to be among the best riders the world has ever known.

Horses are known to be hard workers. In fact, a person who is a hard worker is often called a workhorse.

In America's Old West, horses were preferred to oxen for pulling wagons because horses were both smarter and more willing to try tricky ledges and river crossings. Horses were so important that they became a symbol of the West. In fact, horse thieves, right along with murderers and bank robbers, were hanged for their crime. And horses were essential equipment for sheriffs and deputies. Even today, policemen in cities use horses for crowd control and neighborhood patrols.

What good are horses today?

It seems as if new uses are always being found for horses. Miniature horses, no bigger than Saint Bernards, are gaining popularity as guide animals for the blind. They have one distinct advantage over canine guides—they live two to three times longer than dogs. Horses are also increasingly used in special programs for physically and mentally disabled children and adults, offering them mobility and friendship, and helping them build self-esteem.

Pleasure horses, show horses, and racehorses still make up the bulk of the modern horse population. And even though horses have been replaced by machinery in modern industry, the term used to measure the pulling power of an engine is still *horsepower.*

Horses have amazing physical strength. A pair of Belgian draft horses was able to pull 4,275 pounds (1,941 kg) and set a world record.

Do horses think?

Scientists believe the ability to look into the future and plan ahead shows high-level thinking. Horses don't have long-term goals, but they do think ahead when necessary. A thirsty horse thinks about where to find water, and a horse fed at the same time every day is waiting at the fence when feeding time draws near. A horse has to be able to think to follow his rider's commands.

Experiments have shown that horses can also solve problems. Most horse owners have stories about how one of their horses figured out how to open the latch of his stall or the lid of the feed bin. Horses have also been known to escape pursuit by hiding until the coast is clear and then going the other way. This is called reasoning power, and horses have it.

Horses have another way of thinking. Besides the senses of taste, touch, hearing, sight, and smell, many people credit the horse with an extraordinary sixth sense. This sixth sense allows a horse to detect impending danger and read the moods of his rider.

How do horses learn?

Horses are social animals who live in groups called herds. Every herd has a leader. Horses learn better when trained by a leader figure, so it is a trainer's job to take on the role of leader.

Horses can learn to be good jumpers, but without training, a horse is more likely to walk around something than to jump over it.

Studies have shown that horses respond to gentle and gradual teaching. They are quick to recognize an encouraging tone versus one that is sharp and angry. Screaming at a horse in anger will frighten him and make him harder to control. Talking in soft, calming monotones, on the other hand, can help relax a horse.

Horses respond to sounds like clucking and to words of three syllables or fewer. Commands like *walk on* and *whoa* are easily understood. Horses learn best when a command is accompanied by action. For instance, if you want a horse to move over and you shove him gently as you say "over," the horse gets the idea quickly.

A horse learns gradually, one step at a time. For example, a racehorse is introduced to mechanical starting gates when he is young. First he is walked through a gate, then he stands in the stall with the gate closed, and finally he is urged forward when the gate opens.

Do horses sleep standing up?

They can. A horse's main protection from predators such as wolves and mountain lions is his speed and ability to get off to a quick start. Obviously, a sleeping horse who is standing can take off at the first sign of danger without wasting even a second getting up. Horses have special locking joints at the elbows (at the top of the legs) and the stifles (knees) that allow them to stand and doze. A horse may also sleep propped on his breastbone, a position that allows him to rise quickly.

Horses sleep an average of only four hours a day, taking naps that last about 30 minutes both day and night. A napping horse experiences shortwave sleep (SWS), which the horse can wake from easily. Deep sleep accompanied by rapid eye movement (REM) is dangerous for animals who have to be constantly alert for predators. But horses need REM sleep, too, just like we do. Without it, they become restless and overly tired. In the wild, a herd finds a protected place and posts guards so the other horses can lie down. This allows them to enjoy the relaxation of REM sleep. Like humans, horses probably dream.

Why do some horses wear blinders?

Horses startle easily, just as all prey animals do. They are ready to run at the slightest sign of a threat. A horse can't see far, but he can see all around him—except behind his rump. This is partly because a horse's pupil is a horizontal oval, not a circle, so it gives him a shallow but wide field of vision. And a horse's eyes are set on each side of his head. He can see his rider with a slight turn of the head and look that rider directly in the eye when walking around a bend in a trail.

Blinders help a horse stay focused on what's ahead.

Blinders, also known as blinkers, narrow a horse's field of vision to the same binocular (two-eyed) vision we have. A horse wearing blinders can focus only on the road ahead, which keeps him from becoming alarmed in traffic. Without blinders, a horse might think everything else on the road is chasing him.

Can horses see colors?

Although horses were once believed to be color-blind, new research shows that their cells for seeing color are similar to ours. They see yellow best, followed by orange and red. They can also distinguish green, but have trouble when they get to the blues and violets.

What sounds do horses make?

Horse vocal sounds range from a soft whicker, or nicker, of affection to the bloodcurdling screams of rival stallions clashing. A neigh, the most common horse vocalization, is a fairly loud, high, vibrating noise used to call out to or answer other horses. A whinny is a softer, lower neigh, used to greet a friend, either horse or person. Whinnies can get louder and stronger as a horse gets excited. Squeals are short, sharp blasts of sound, usually indicating sudden pain or fear. However,

colts use squeals when playing, especially during mock battles. A horse suffering from illness or overexertion may groan or grunt.

How many different breeds of horses are there?

Experts disagree on the total number of horse breeds, but the American Horse Council recognizes 114 breeds of horses in the U.S. Many of them were developed in a particular region. For example, the quarter horse and paint horse were developed in North America, and the barb and Arabian were developed in the Middle East and Africa.

All breeds fall into three categories: coldbloods, hotbloods, and warmbloods, which have nothing to do with the temperature of a horse's blood. All horses have an average temperature of about 99–101 degrees Fahrenheit (37.2–38.3 degrees Celsius). Coldbloods are large, heavy horses, with a high level of endurance and the ability to work hard. Hotbloods are the fastest of all horses. Originally bred to live in hot desert climates, hotbloods include both Arabians and Thoroughbreds. These horses tend to be fiery, proud, and spirited. Warmbloods, the largest category, are breeds developed from hotbloods and coldbloods for special uses. Warmbloods tend to have spirit and stamina but are more responsive than hotbloods to human direction.

In America, the dominant breeds are the quarter horse, mustang, Morgan, Thoroughbred, and standardbred.

How many colors of horses are there?

You might as well ask how many shapes of snowflakes there are. Horses come in a seemingly endless number of colors, markings, and combinations. This is why subtly different colors and patterns have been given their own names such as chestnut, sorrel, dun, strawberry roan, bay, dapple gray, liver, buckskin, piebald, skewbald, cremello, and palomino. The dapple gray, for example, has dark gray rings on a light gray coat and a gray mane and tail. The chestnut, also called sorrel, has a reddish gold coat, mane,

and tail. The palomino has a golden coat with a white mane and tail. In fact, horses come in so many different colors and markings that there are official color registries, or record books, that are separate from the breed registries.

White marks on a horse's face are described as stripes, blazes, stars, or snips. White markings on the legs just above the hooves can be long (socks), medium (white pastern), or narrow (white coronet). There are few true albino horses, who have pink eyes. Pure white horses usually have blue eyes or they may be walleyed, with one brown and one blue eye.

Some sources claim
that miniatures have
been as small as
3 or 4 hands, but
Shetland ponies are
usually 9 hands.

What are the biggest and the smallest horses?

Horses arrived on the scene long before the metric system or yardstick were invented, so a uniform way of measuring the animal had to be found. Hands are easily accessible (most people have two handy!) so they became the units used to measure horses. On average, an adult human hand is 4 inches (10.2 cm) wide. Measurements are made from the bottom of the hoof to the withers at the base of a horse's neck.

Draft horses such as the Belgian, the Percheron, the Clydesdale, the Suffolk punch, and the shire are the biggest. Among draft horses, the ancient shire is considered the biggest of all. It stands about 18 hands, which is 6 feet (1.8 m) tall, from hoof to withers.

Modern miniature, or dwarf, horses were first developed in the late nineteenth century by the Falabella family of Argentina. The initial miniatures came from crossing a Shetland pony with a freakishly small Thoroughbred. People bred these small horses to each other to produce even smaller horses. Unfortunately, through this continuous inbreeding, miniature horses developed some physical weaknesses.

Many people keep miniature horses as pets, treating them much as they would a dog. They lack the Shetland pony's strength so only a small child can ride them.

Sources differ as to who are the biggest and the smallest horses. *Guinness World Records 2004* gives the honor of biggest horse to a British shire named Samson. He measured 21.3

hands, which is just over 7 feet (2.1 m). *Guinness World Records 2001* is the most recent year that includes the smallest horse category, and it gives that honor to a mare named Black Beauty, who is 4.6 hands, which is 18.5 inches (47 cm). She was born in 1996 on the Burleson Arabian Horse Farm in Kittrell, North Carolina, and spends most of her time in the Burlesons' house, where she likes to watch TV and eat popcorn.

Before machines, draft horses were commonly used for transportation, construction, and agriculture.

What's the difference between a pony, a donkey, and a mule?

A pony is a type of horse. There are over 30 breeds of ponies, including the Scottish Shetland, the Norwegian fjord, the Italian Bardigiano, the Irish Connemara, the British dales, the Russian Bashkir curly, and the American Chincoteague. Strong, compact pony breeds vary in size, but they usually stay under 14.2 hands, which is 56.7 inches (1.4 m). Unlike most horses, whose height is greater than their length, ponies (and many draft horses) are longer than they are tall.

Both donkeys and mules are in the same equine family as the horse. Donkeys, also called burros, have been around since ancient times and were used mainly as pack animals. They are scrubby, have a loud heehaw, and are

Donkey

probably pound for pound the hardest working animal in the world.

A mule has a donkey father and a horse mother. A hinny (sometimes called a jennet) has a horse father and a donkey mother. Mules and hinnies were developed to combine the donkey's stamina with the horse's strength. With few exceptions, mules and hinnies produce no offspring.

Mule

Pony

What kind of horse is a bucking bronco?

Horse experts suspect the bucking instinct developed in wild mustangs of the Argentine prairie and the Western plains. These horses were often attacked by mountain lions and other wild cats. Once a horse is attacked, his only possible defense against a wild cat is to try to buck it off. Such attacks were so common that these wild mustangs developed a lifesaving instinct to buck off any animal who tried to mount them. Training a wild mustang became an endurance contest between horse and human, and a popular attraction at rodeos.

A bucking bronco lowers his head, humps his back, and leaps in the air like a stiff-legged rabbit. He also sways and then stands on his forelegs and tries to pitch the rider off. With training, most broncs keep bucking for only a day or two before settling down into regular saddle horses. The Mexicans call the ones who never settle down *potro bronco,* or wild horse.

Are there any wild horses left today?

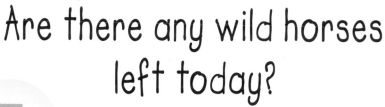

There are no breeds of wild horses that exist today. Herds of horses run wild in the American West and Australia, but they are feral horses, who were once domestic but have returned to a wild state. The tarpan, native to Poland and Russia, was one of the last wild horses. Unfortunately, its meat was considered to be delicious. By the end of the nineteenth century, it had been hunted nearly to extinction. Despite heroic attempts to save it, the last wild tarpan died in 1879. Through conservation programs, a tarpan-type horse has been restored and a small herd now roams the Bialowieski Forest in Poland.

The Mongolian wild horse was the last true wild horse. It hasn't been seen in the wild since the 1960s. It can now be seen in zoos, where it is called the Przewalski's horse after the Englishman who brought the horse to Western Europe. There are about 1,100 left in zoos today. Unfortunately, the Mongolian wild horse died out the same way the tarpan did. People considered its meat a delicacy.

Once upon a time, all horses were wild. Today there are no truly wild breeds left.

Why do horses roll on the ground?

Mostly because it feels good! It also helps horses shed their long, thick winter coat. And it gets rid of dandruff by helping shed skin flakes. Rolling also covers the coat with dust or mud, which helps protect horses from flies and other insects.

What is a horsefly?

Flies can be a big problem for horses, who sometimes develop allergies to fly bites. There are over 16,000 types of flies, but only a few of them actually bite. With horseflies, only the female bites and sucks blood; the male drinks nectar from flowers. Horseflies are named for their size, not for their attraction to horses (although they do bite horses). A horsefly can be 3 to 10 times bigger than the common housefly.

This foal is being "bugged" by something. Horses use their tails to swish away flies, and their teeth to scratch an itch.

Why do horses wear shoes?

A horse's hooves are protected on the outside by horn, a form of skin much like the human fingernail. Like our nails, hoof horn grows all the time. It gets worn down when a horse walks on hard surfaces. Horses wear metal shoes to prevent their hoof horns from wearing down unevenly, to protect their feet from stones, and to help angle each foot for a steadier gait.

A farrier is someone who specializes in shoeing horses. Since a shoe prevents the horn from being worn down, a farrier has to trim away excess horn every one to two months at each shoe refitting. It takes a horse, on average, one year to grow a completely new hoof horn.

Shoes are routinely worn by most horses. Feral horses, who run wild, don't wear shoes. And a few other breeds that are not far removed from their wild ancestors, like Dartmoor ponies and Nokota horses, don't need shoes because their hooves are so hard.

Legend has it that horseshoes bring good luck. Some people hang them above doorways, upside down so the luck won't run out.

What is a gait?

It's not the part of a fence that opens; it's the way a horse moves. A horse has three basic natural gaits: the walk; the trot, or jog; and the canter, or lope. Some people count the gallop as a fourth gait, but it's really a fast canter. People teach horses specialized gaits such as the pace (used in harness racing), the amble (a broken rhythm gait used mainly by Icelandic ponies), and the rack (a flashy fast walk with great flexing and lifting of the knees).

The walk, the slowest natural gait, has four beats, with each foot hitting the ground separately. The trot has two beats: left hind and right fore together, then right hind and left fore together. The canter has three beats: left hind; left fore and right hind together; and right fore. The added speed of the gallop gives a horse more time suspended in the air with all four feet off the ground.

How fast can a horse run?

Some experts consider Kentucky Thoroughbreds to be the fastest horses in the world. They can race at speeds up to 45 miles per hour (72.4 kph), and cover more than 20 feet (6.1 m) in a single stride. These horses have an amazing arc of flight, the amount of time all four feet are off the ground. The Kentucky Thoroughbred began building up speed way back in 1775, when Daniel Boone presented the first Kentucky legislature with a bill for improving Kentucky horses.

A horse moves two to three times faster at a gallop than at a canter.

Why are all Thoroughbreds given January 1 as their birth date?

Most Thoroughbreds are born in January, but Thoroughbreds become a year older on January 1 no matter when they were actually born. Their birthdays are standardized for ease in record-keeping, an important function in the racing world. So a Thoroughbred born in late December is considered, for racing purposes, to be one year old the following month.

A number of other factors contribute to this rather odd custom. Since Thoroughbreds are so fast, they are pushed to get off to a fast start in life, too. Thoroughbreds typically begin working out as yearlings, or one-year-olds. They move on to professional racing as two-year-olds. Most Thoroughbreds are retired from racing by the time they're five—the age when other saddle horses are just starting their careers. Because Thoroughbreds are believed to peak so early, they are actually bred to mature early.

A racing Thoroughbred can reach speeds up to 40 miles per hour (64 kph).

Do people shoot horses with a broken leg?

The answer 20 years ago would have been yes. Equine legs are too big and carry too much weight for casting alone to work. Luckily, many fine equine veterinarians and hospitals exist today, and surgery and casting are now possible. Modern veterinarians can perform a delicate procedure using a stabilizing plate and screen to keep the leg bones together. In addition, horses can be given metal leg implants.

Today, most types of breaks can be treated, but it's usually costly and complicated.

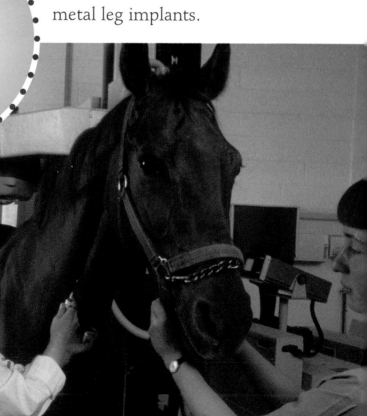

What happens to old horses?

Old horses today never go to the glue factory, although they may have a century ago. Natural glue is now made mostly from the skin, bones, and hooves of cattle, all by-products of the beef industry. Unwanted and aging horses do, however, often go to the slaughterhouse. Their meat is sold for human consumption in parts of Europe and Japan and made into dog food; their powdered hooves are used to make gelatin.

In Kentucky, home to America's best-known horse race, the Kentucky Derby, champion horses are buried in caskets, and their graves are marked with a headstone.

How old do horses live to be?

Horses stop growing at around the age of 5. They are considered mature between 6 and 7 years of age. And horses over the age of 20 are usually considered senior citizens. The oldest horse in recorded history is Old Billy, an English barge horse who was born in 1760 and died in 1822 at the age of 62. Most horses, though, live for 25 to 35 years.

A horse's age can be determined by his teeth. Horses have big teeth that push forward and change shape from oval to round to triangular to flat as they age. These worn teeth also become discolored. The upper incisors develop a mark called Galvayne's groove when a horse is around 10 years old. As a horse ages, the groove continues to expand downward, usually extending all the way to the end of the tooth by the time a horse is 20.

Tartar is also a common ailment in older horses and must be scraped or chipped off to avoid gum disorders. Because a horse's gums tend to recede with age, more and more tooth shows, thus the phrase "long in the tooth," used to describe an old horse (or person!).

Who are the most famous horses in the world?

Back in the 1940s and 1950s, cowboy movies and TV shows were America's most popular form of entertainment. There were a lot of famous horses during that time. The Lone Ranger rode Silver. Gene Autry rode Champion. Roy Rogers's palomino, Trigger, was a star of both movies and TV. When Trigger died, Rogers had him stuffed by a taxidermist and put on display in the Roy Rogers-Dale Evans Museum, which is now in Branson, Missouri.

Horses like Black Beauty and Misty of Chincoteague became famous in books that are still widely read. And real-life horses are now becoming famous by way of the movies. The movie *Hidalgo* tells the incredible story of cowboy Frank T. Hopkins and his little mustang who entered a grueling 3,000-mile (4,827-km) Arabian endurance race in the 1890s. Hidalgo, who was considered to be the underdog, reached the finish line more than a day ahead of the other horses. *Seabiscuit,* another recent horse film about an underdog, recalls the unlikely career of a misfit racehorse who won against impossible odds.

But no mention of modern horse fame would be complete without Secretariat (1970–1989), Seattle Slew (1974–2002), and Affirmed (1975–2001). Secretariat won America's three top races—the Kentucky Derby, the Preakness, and the Belmont Stakes—to win the Triple Crown in 1973, 25 years after the last horse won it. Seattle Slew took the Crown in 1977, and Affirmed won it the very next year, in 1978.

Famous or not, horses have been the subject of poems, stories, and songs throughout history. And expressions like "you can lead a horse to water, but you can't make him drink" are commonplace today. American poet James Whitcomb Riley may have captured our feelings for the horse best when he wrote, "I love the horse from hoof to head, from head to hoof and tail to mane, I love the horse, as I have said, from head to hoof and back again."

From ancient times,
to the Old West, to today, horses have been
an important part of our lives.

straight from the horse's mouth

This phrase is used to mean getting your facts straight and knowing what's what. Here are some amazing facts, straight from the horse's mouth:

- The large dapple gray Percheron is known as the rosinback in the circus. This horse has such a steady gait that a ballerina can dance on its broad back once its been rubbed with a nonslip powder called rosin to give the dancer traction.

- In 1976, during this nation's bicentennial, "The Great American Horse Race" was held, starting in Sacramento, California, and ending in New York City. One hundred entrants left the starting line on Memorial Day. The winner crossed the finish line on Labor Day. He was a farmer named Vero Norton, and he was riding a mule.

- Photographer Eadweard Muybridge was asked in 1872 by the governor of California to prove whether or not racehorses ever had ALL four feet off the ground at once. He set up a row of cameras and connected them to clocks, aiming for a snapshot every 1/6,000 of a second. His experiment proved that all four of a racehorse's feet do leave the ground at two points in every stride. Muybridge thus invented stop-action photography, which has been used since 1888 to record photo finishes.

resources

BOOKS

BUDD, JACKIE. *Horses.* New York: Kingfisher, 1995.

BUDIANSKY, STEPHEN. *The World According to Horses: How They Run, See, and Think.* New York: Henry Holt & Company, 2000.

CLUTTON-BROCK, JULIET. *Horse.* New York: Alfred A. Knopf, 1992.

COOPER, JILLY. *Animals in War.* London: William Heinmann Ltd., 2002.

EDWARDS, ELWYN HARTLEY. *Ultimate Horse.* New York: DK Publishing Inc., 2002.

EVANS, EDNA H. *Famous Horses and Their People.* Brattleboro, Vermont: The Stephen Green Press, 1975.

HARRIS, SARAH. *Factfinder Guide: Horses.* London: PRC Publishing Ltd., 1999.

JACKSON, JAMIE. *Natural Horse: Lessons from the Wild for Domestic Horse Care.* Flagstaff, Arizona: Northland Pub., 1992.

KIMBALL, CHERYL. *The Everything Horse Book.* Avon, Mass.: Adams Media Corp., 2001.

KLIMO, KATE. *Heroic Horses and their Riders.* New York: Platt & Munk Publishers, 1974.

MACGREGOR-MORRIS, PAMELA, et al. *The Book of the Horse.* New York: Exeter Books, 1979.

MCBANE, SUSAN, and HELEN DOUGLAS-COOPER. *Horse Facts.* London: Quantum Books Ltd., 1991.

MERRIMAN, JOHN M., ED. *For Want of a Horse.* New York: Viking Penguin Inc., 1985.

PAVIA, AUDREY. *Horses for Dummies.* New York: Hungry Minds, Inc., 1999.

PRICE, STEVEN D., et al. *The Whole Horse Catalog, Revised and Updated.* New York: Simon & Schuster, 1998.

SCANLON, LAWRENCE. *Wild About Horses: Our Timeless Passion for the Horse.* New York: HarperCollins, 1998.

SMITH, ELINOR GOULDING. *Horses, History, and Havoc.* Cleveland, Ohio: The World Publishing Co., 1969.

TUCKER, LOUISE. *The Visual Dictionary of the Horse.* New York: DK Publishing Inc., 1994.

VERNON, ARTHUR. *The History and Romance of the Horse.* New York: Dover Publications, 1946.

WEXO, JOHN BONNETT. *Zoobooks Wild Horses.* San Diego, California: Wildlife Education, Ltd., 1987.

WEB SITES

www.equinenet.org
This is a good all-around Web site on horses, including information on horse heroes.

www.factmonster.com/spot/01triplecrown1.html
This Web site covers racing and the Triple Crown in a way that is fun and understandable for kids.

www.guidehorse.org
Find out about miniature horses who guide the blind by logging onto this Web site.

www.historyforkids.org/learn/environment/horses.htm
Log onto this kid-friendly Web site to learn all about the history of horses.

www.horsefun.com
This is a fun-filled Web site where horse lovers can work puzzles, test their horse knowledge, and learn amazing horse facts.

www.horses4kids.com
This Web site has games, quizzes, and stories, among other fun horse activities.

www.horseworldwide.com
Click on Kids Especially to find links to games, quizzes, contests, clubs, and other horsey activities.

www.kidsdomain.com/kids/links/Horses.html
Log onto this resource page to find links to PBS documentaries about horses; horse fossils from the Florida Museum of Natural History; plus puzzles, kids' poetry, and more.

www.kidstothecup.com
This kid-friendly Web site offers a good introduction to horse racing and its challenges.

www.wildhorse.com
This Web site has links to many horse resources for everything from art and poetry to films and TV.

About the Author

MARTY CRISP loves animals. She's written 17 books, including Kids' FAQs books about dogs, cats, dolphins, and now horses. She lives in Pennsylvania Dutch Country, where horse-and-buggies drive the roads and horses plow the fields. Ms. Crisp has also written many books about dog adventures, and she lives in a "pack" of five: herself, her husband, a Cavalier King Charles spaniel, a Yorkshire terrier, and a cairn terrier. The dogs in the Crisp pack are certain they're in charge, and they might just be right!

Besides animals, Ms. Crisp also loves kids and doing everything kids do, except not getting to eat all the ice cream you want and having your mom make you dust. You can find out more about the author at her Web site, **www.martycrisp.com.**

Do you have questions about other animals? We want to hear from you! E-mail us at **kidsfaqs@tnkidsbooks.com.** For more details, log on to **www.tnkidsbooks.com.**